JAMES FRANCO

Frank Bidart

METAPHYSICAL DOG

Frank Bidart's most recent full-length collections of poetry are *Watching the Spring Festival* (FSG, 2008), *Star Dust* (FSG, 2005), *Desire* (FSG, 1997), and *In the Western Night: Collected Poems 1965–90* (FSG, 1990). He has won many prizes, including the Wallace Stevens Award and, most recently, the 2007 Bollingen Prize for Poetry. He teaches at Wellesley College.

METAPHYSICAL DOG

Frank Bidart

Farrar, Straus and Giroux

New York

Farrar, Straus and Giroux
18 West 18th Street, New York 10011

Printed in the United States of America
Published in 2013 by Farrar, Straus and Giroux
First paperback edition, 2014

Poems from this book have appeared, sometimes in earlier
versions, in The New Republic, The New Yorker, Salmagundi,
Slate, The Threepenny Review, Tin House, and The Wolf.
"Interview with Frank Bidart" by Shara Lessley is reprinted
with the kind permission of the National Book Foundation.

The Library of Congress has cataloged
the hardcover edition as follows:
Bidart, Frank, 1939–
    [Poems. Selections]
    Metaphysical dog / Frank Bidart. — First edition.
      pages cm
    Poems.
    ISBN 978-0-374-17361-6 (alk. paper)
    I. Title.

PS3552.I33 M48 2013
811'.54—dc23

                                    2012048069

Paperback ISBN: 978-0-374-53462-2

www.fsgbooks.com
www.twitter.com/fsgbooks
www.facebook.com/fsgbooks

10 9 8 7 6 5 4 3 2 1

CONTENTS

One

Two: Hunger for the Absolute

Three: History is a series of failed revelations

Four

Five

ONE

METAPHYSICAL DOG

Belafont, who reproduced what we did
not as an act of supine

imitation, but in defiance—

butt on couch and front legs straddling
space to rest on an ottoman, barking till

his masters clean his teeth with dental floss.

How dare being
give him this body.

Held up to a mirror, he writhed.

was exorcism.

•

Exorcism of that thing within Frank that wanted, after his mother's death, to die.

•

Inside him was that thing that he must expel from him to live.

•

He read "The Case of Ellen West" as a senior in college and immediately wanted to write a poem about it but couldn't so he stored it, as he has stored so much that awaits existence.

•

Unlike Ellen he was never anorexic but like Ellen he was obsessed with eating and the arbitrariness of gender and having to have a body.

•

Ellen lived out the war between the mind and the body, lived out in her body each stage of the war, its journey and progress, in which compromise, reconciliation is attempted then rejected then mourned, till she reaches at last, in an ecstasy costing not less than everything, death.

.

He was grateful he was not impelled to live out the war in his body, hiding in compromise, well wadded with art he adored and with stupidity and distraction.

.

The particularity inherent in almost all narrative, though contingent and exhausting, tells the story of the encounter with particularity that flesh as flesh must make.

.

"Ellen West" was written in the year after his mother's death.

.

By the time she died he had so thoroughly betrayed the ground of intimacy on which his life was founded he had no right to live.

.

No use for him to tell himself that he shouldn't feel this because he felt this.

·

He didn't think this but he thought this.

·

After she died his body wanted to die, but his brain, his cunning, didn't.

·

He likes narratives with plots that feel as if no one willed them.

·

His mother in her last year revealed that she wanted him to move back to Bakersfield and teach at Bakersfield College and live down the block.

·

He thought his mother, without knowing that this is what she wanted, wanted him to die.

·

All he had told her in words and more than words for years was that her possessiveness and terror at his independence were wrong, wrong, wrong.

•

He was the only person she wanted to be with but he refused to live down the block and then she died.

•

It must be lifted from the mind

must be lifted and placed elsewhere
must not remain in the mind alone

•

Out of the thousand myriad voices, thousand myriad stories in each human head, when his mother died, there was Ellen West.

•

This is the body that you can draw out of you to expel from you the desire to die.

•

Give it a voice, give each scene of her life a particularity and necessity that in Binswanger's recital are absent.

•

Enter her skin so that you can then make her other and expel her.

•

Survive her.

•

Animal mind, eating the ground of Western thought, the "mind-body" problem.

•

She, who in the last months of her life abandoned writing poems in disgust at the failure of her poems, is a poem.

•

She in death is incarnated on a journey whose voice is the voice of her journey.

•

Arrogance of Plutarch, of Shakespeare and Berlioz, who thought they made what Cleopatra herself could not make.

•

Arrogance of the maker.

•

Werther killed himself and then young men all over Europe imitated him and killed themselves but his author, Goethe, cunning master of praxis, lived.

.

Frank thought when anything is made it is made not by its likeness, not by its twin or mirror, but its opposite.

.

Ellen in his poem asks *Without a body, who can* know *himself at all?*

.

In your pajamas, you moved down the stairs just to the point where the adults couldn't yet see you, to hear more clearly the din, the sweet cacophony of adults partying.

.

Phonograph voices among them, phonograph voices, their magpie beauty.

.

Sweet din.

.

Magpie beauty.

•

One more poem, one more book in which you figure out how to make something out of not knowing enough.

LIKE

Woe is blunted not erased
by *like*. Your hands were too full, then

empty. At the grave's

lip, secretly you imagine then
refuse to imagine

a spectre

so like what you watched die, the unique
soul you loved endures a second death.

The dead hate *like*, bitter

when the living with too-small
grief replace them. You dread

loving again, exhausted by the hungers

ineradicable in his presence. *You resist*
strangers until a stranger makes the old hungers

brutally wake. We live by symbolic

substitution. At the grave's lip, what is
but is not is what

returns you to what is not.

TWO

Hunger for the Absolute

THOSE NIGHTS

Those nights when despite his exhaustion or indifference
you persisted, then finally it

caught, so that at last he too

wanted it, suddenly was desperate to reach it,
you felt his muscles want it

more than anything, as if through this chaos, this

wilderness he again knew the one thing he must reach
though later, after

he found it, his resentment implied he had been forced.

•

Those nights ended because what was
missing could never be by
the will supplied. We who could get
somewhere through
words through
sex could not. I was, you said, your
shrink: that's how
I held you. I failed as my own.

•

Now you surely are dead. I've searched
the databases: you everywhere
elude us. Long ago without your
reaching to tell me, surely
the plague killed you. Each thing in your life
you found so
incommensurate to the spirit
I imagine that becoming
untraceable makes you smile.

NAME THE BED

Halflight just after dawn. As you turned back
in the doorway, you to whom the ordinary

sensuous world seldom speaks

expected to see in the thrown-off
rumpled bedclothes nothing.

.

Scream stretched across it.

.

Someone wanted more from that bed
than was found there.

.

Name the bed that's not true of.

.

Bed where your twin
died. Eraser bed.

QUEER

Lie to yourself about this and you will
forever lie about everything.

Everybody already knows everything

so you can
lie to them. That's what they want.

But lie to yourself, what you will

lose is yourself. Then you
turn into them.

●

For each gay kid whose adolescence

was America in the forties or fifties
the primary, the crucial

scenario

forever is coming out—
or not. Or not. Or not. Or not. Or not.

●

Involuted velleities of self-erasure.

.

Quickly after my parents
died, I came out. Foundational narrative

designed to confer existence.

If I had managed to come out to my
mother, she would have blamed not

me, but herself.

*The door through which you were shoved out
into the light*

was self-loathing and terror.

.

Thank you, terror!

You learned early that adults' genteel
fantasies about human life

were not, for you, life. You think sex

is a knife
driven into you to teach you that.

HISTORY

For two years, my father chose to live at

The Bakersfield Inn, which called itself
the largest motel in the world.

There, surrounded by metal furniture

painted to look like wood, I told him that I
wanted to be a priest, a Trappist.

He asked how I could live without pussy.

He asked this earnestly. This confession
of what he perceived as need

was generous. I could not tell him.

●

Sex shouldn't be part of marriage.

Your father and I, —
. . . sex shouldn't be part of marriage.

●

That she loved and continued to love him
alone: and he, her: even after marrying others—

then they got old and stopped talking this way.

.

Ecstasy in your surrender to adolescent

God-hunger, ecstasy
promised by obliterated sex, ecstasy

in which you are free because bound—

in which you call the God who made
what must be obliterated in you love.

.

In a labyrinth of blankets in the garage

at seven
with a neighbor boy

you learned abasement

learned amazed that what must be
obliterated in you is the twisted

obverse of what underlies everything.

•

Chaos of love, chaos of sex that
marriage did not solve or

mask, God did not solve or mask.

•

Grant and Hepburn in *Bringing Up Baby*,

in which Grant finally realizes being
with her is more fun than anything.

•

What they left behind

they left behind
broken. The fiction

even they accepted, even they believed

was that once
it was whole.

Once it was whole

left all who swallowed it,
however skeptical, forever hungry.

•

The generation that followed, just like their
famished parents, fell in love with the fiction.

They smeared shit all over

their inheritance because it was broken,
because they fell in love with it.

But I had found my work.

HUNGER FOR THE ABSOLUTE

Earth you know is round but seéms flat.

You can't trust
your senses.

You thought you had seen every variety of creature
but not

this creature.

.

When I met him, I knew I had

weaned myself from God, not
hunger for the absolute. O unquenched

mouth, tonguing what is and must
remain inapprehensible —

saying *You are not finite. You are not finite.*

DEFROCKED

Christ the bridegroom, the briefly
almost-satiated soul forever then

the bride—

the true language of ecstasy
is the forbidden

language of the mystics:

I am true love that false was never.

      I would be pierced
And I would pierce

      I would eat
And I would be eaten

I am peace that is nowhere in time.

Naked their
encounter with the absolute,—

pilgrimage to a cross in the void.

A journey you still must travel, for
which you have no language

since you no longer believe it exists.

•

When what we understand about
what we are

changes, whole
parts of us fall mute.

•

We have attached sensors to your most intimate

body parts, so that we may measure
what you think, not what you think you think.
The image now on the screen
will circumvent your superego and directly stimulate your

vagina or dick

or fail to. Writing has existed for centuries to tell us
what you think you think. Liar,
we are interested in what lies
beneath that. This won't hurt.

•

Even in lawless dreams, something
each night in me again

denies me

the false coin, false
creature I crave to embrace—

for those milliseconds, not

false. Not false. Even if false,
the waters of paradise

are there, in the mind, the sleeping

mind. *Why this puritan each
night inside me that again denies me.*

•

Chimeras glitter: fierce energy you
envy.

Chimeras ignorant they're chimeras
beckon.

As you reach into their crotch, they foretell
your fate.

With a sudden rush of milk you taste
what has

no end.

.

We long for the Absolute, Royce
said. Voices you once

heard that you can never *not* hear again, —

. . . spoiled priest, liar, if you want something
enough, sometimes you think it's there.

HE IS AVA GARDNER

He is Ava Gardner at the height of her beauty
in *Pandora and the Flying Dutchman.*

I had allowed him to become, for me, necessity.
I was not ever for him necessity.

An adornment, yes. A grace-note. Not
necessity.

Everyone, the men at least, are crazy about
Pandora. She is smart,

self-deprecating, funny. She who has seen,
seemingly, everything about love, and says

she has no idea what love is—
who knows the world finds her beautiful, so that

she must test every man and slightly disgusted
find him wanting—clearly she has not, in this

crowd of men eager to please her, to flatter
and bring her drinks, found someone

who is, for her, necessity. Watching
Pandora and the Flying Dutchman, you feel sympathy

for the beautiful
who cannot find anyone who is for them necessity.

                    •

He is Ava Gardner
at the height of her beauty.

Fucked up, you knew you'd never fall for someone
not fucked up.

You watch her test each suitor. She sings about
love to an old friend, drunk, a poet.

He asks her to marry him. After she again
refuses, you see him slip something into his drink—

then he dies, poisoned. She says he has tried that
too many times, now she feels nothing.

Promising nothing, she asks the famous
race-car driver, who also wants to marry her,

to shove the car he has worked on for months
over the cliff, into the sea. He

does. In the first flush of
pleasure, she agrees to marry him. The next day

he has the car's
carcass, pouring water, dragged up from the sea.

You are the learned, amused professor surrounded
by his collections, who carefully pieces together

fragments of Greek pots. You know it is foolish
to become another suitor. *Hors de*

combat, soon you are the only one she trusts.
You become, at moments, her confessor.

.

Then she meets the Dutchman.
He offers little, asks nothing.

When she withdraws her
attention, he isn't spooked.

Because, when she meets him, he is
painting the portrait of someone who has

her face, with petulance
she scrapes off the face.

He charmingly makes her head a blank
ovoid, and says that's better.

She thinks that she is the knife
that, cutting him, will heal him.

.

You know she is right. You have discovered
he is the fabled Dutchman — who for

centuries has sailed the world's seas
unable to die, unable to die though

he wants to die. You know what it is to
want to die. His reasons

are a little contrived, a mechanism of the plot:
reasons that Pandora, at the end, discovers:

he murdered, centuries earlier, through
jealousy and paranoia, his wife: now

unless he can find a woman
willing to die

out of love for him, sail out with him
and drown, he cannot ever

find rest. This logic
makes sense to her: she who does not

believe in love
will perform an act proving its existence.

•

She wants, of course, to throw her life away.
The Dutchman will always arrive

because that's what she wants.
Those of us who look on, who want

the proximate and partial to continue,
loathe the hunger for the absolute.

•

All your life you have watched as two creatures
think they have found in each other

necessity. Watched as the shell
then closes, for a time, around them.

You envy them, as you gather with
the rest of the village, staring out to sea.

When she swims out to his boat, to give
herself, both succeed at last in drowning.

•

Couples stay together when each of the two
remains a necessity for the other. Which you

cannot know, until they
cease to be. Tautology

that is the sum of what you know.
He is a master, he has lived by

becoming the master
of the alchemy that makes, as you

stare into some one
person's eyes, makes you adore him.

Eyes that say that despite the enormous
landscapes that divide you

you are brothers, he too is trapped in
all that divides soul from soul. Then

suddenly he is fluttering his finger ends
between yours. He rises

from the table, explains he had no
sleep last night, and leaves.

                    •

You couldn't worm your way into
becoming, for him, necessity.

When did he grow bored with seduction and
confessors, and find the Dutchman?—

For months there has been nothing
but silence. When you sent him a pot only

you could have with care pieced together
from the catastrophe of history, more

silence. *The enterprise is abandoned.*

.

Something there is in me that makes me
think I need this thing. That gives this thing

the illusion of necessity.

As enthralled to flesh
as I, he could not see beneath this old

face I now wear, this ruinous, ugly
body, that I

I am the Dutchman.

But nobody knows, when living, where
necessity lies. Maybe later, if history

is lucky, the urn
will not refuse to be pieced together.

This is neither good nor bad.
It is what is.

MOURN

Why so hard
to give up

what often
was ever

even then
hardly there.

But the safe
world my will

constructed
before him

this soul could
not find breath

in. He brought
electric

promise-crammed
sudden air.

Then withdrew
lazily

as if to
teach you how

you must live
short of breath.

Still now crave
sudden air.

THE ENTERPRISE IS ABANDONED.

I'm not a fool, I knew from the beginning
what couldn't happen. What couldn't happen

didn't. *The enterprise is abandoned.*

But half our life is
dreams, delirium, everything that underlies

that feeds

that keeps alive the illusion of sanity, semi-
sanity, we allow

others to see. The half of me that feeds the rest

is in mourning. Mourns. Each time we must
mourn, we fear this is the final mourning, this time

mourning never will lift. A friend said when a lover

dies, it takes
two years. Then it lifts.

Inside those two years, you punish

not only the world,
but yourself.

At seventy-two, the future is what I mourn.

Since college I've never forgotten Masha
in *The Seagull* saying *I am in mourning for my life.*

She wears only black, she treats others with

fierce solicitude
and sudden punishment.

The enterprise is abandoned. And not.

JANÁČEK AT SEVENTY

It was merely a locket but it was
a locket only

I could have made —

Once she is told that it was made
for her, recognizes it as a locket

her little agile famous-in-his-little-world

Vulcan
himself

made only for her, she must

reach for it, must
place it around her neck.

Soon the warmth of her flesh

must warm what I have made.
Her husband will know who made it

so she will wear it

only when
alone, but wear it she will.

THRENODY ON THE DEATH OF HARRIET SMITHSON

She was barely twenty, she was called
Miss Smithson, but through her

Juliet, Desdemona

found superb utterance. A new
truth, Shakespeare's old truth

bewitched us, unheard

until she made us hear it—she
heralded a revolution

Madame Dorval, Lemaître, Malibran,

yes, Victor Hugo
and Berlioz

then taught us we had always known.

Now, at fifty-four, she is dead,—
. . . bitter that fame long ago abandoned her.

I think her fate our fate, the planet's fate.

•

These fleeting creatures, that flit by
giving themselves to us

and the air

unable to etch there
anything permanent

Addicted to the ecstasies of

carving again from darkness
a shape, an illusion of light

They say, *I wash my hands of the gods*

this has existed
whether the whirling planet tomorrow

survive, whether recording angels exist

•

On this stage at this
moment *this* has existed

unerasable because already erased

Everything finally, of course, is
metaphysical

this has existed

THREE

History is a series of

failed revelations

DREAM OF THE BOOK

That great hopefulness that lies in
imagining you are an unreadable, not

blank slate, but something even you cannot

read because words will rise from its
depths only when you at last

manage to expose it to air, —

the pathology of the provinces. *You need
air.*

·

Then you find air. Somehow somewhere

as if whatever feeds expectation were
wounded, gutted by the bewildering self-

buried thousand impersonations

by which you know you
made and remade

yourself, —

one day, staring at the mountain,
you ceased to ask

Open Sesame

merely requiring that narrative reveal
something structural about the world.

•

Reading history

you learn that those who cannot read
history are condemned to repeat it

etcetera

just like those who
can, or think they can.

Substitute the psyche for history   substitute myth for

the psyche   economics
for myth   substitute politics, culture, history etc.

•

As if there were a book

As if there were a book inside which you can
breathe

Where, at every turn, you see at last the lineaments

Where the end of the earth's long dream of
virtue is *not*, as you have

again and again found it here, the will

gazing out at the dilemmas
proceeding from its own nature

unbroken but in stasis

•

Seduced not by a book but by the idea
of a book

like the *Summa* in five fat volumes, that your priest

in high school explained Thomas Aquinas
almost finished, except that there were,

maddeningly, "just a few things he didn't

have time, before dying, quite
to figure out"

•

That history is a series of failed revelations

you're sure you hear folded, hidden
within the all-but-explicit

bitter

taste-like-dirt inside Dinah Washington's
voice singing *This bitter earth*

•

A few months before Thomas'

death, as he talked with Jesus
Jesus asked him

what reward he wanted for his

virtue —
to which Thomas replied, *You, Lord,*

only You —

which is why, as if this vision
unfit him for his life, he told the priest

prodding him to take up once again

writing his book, *Reginald, I cannot:*
everything I have written I now see is straw.

·

Though the Book whose text articulates

the text of
creation

is an arrogance, you think, flung by priests

at all that is
fecund, that has not yet found being

Though priests, addicted to

unanswerable but necessary questions,
also everywhere are addicted to cruel answers

you wake happy

when you dream
you have seen the book, the Book exists

·

You sail protested, contested
seas, the something within you that

chooses your masters

itself not chosen. Inheritor inheriting
inheritors, you must earn what you inherit.

INAUGURATION DAY

(JANUARY 20, 2009)

Today, despite what is dead

staring out across America I see since
Lincoln gunmen
nursing fantasies of purity betrayed,
dreaming to restore
the glories of their blood and state

despite what is dead but lodged within us, hope

under the lustrous flooding moon
the White House is still
Whitman's White House, its
gorgeous front
full of reality, full of illusion

hope made wise by dread begins again

RACE

(FOR LEON WOOD, JR.)

America is ours
to ruin but
not ours to dream.

The unstained but
terrifying land
Europe imagined

soon the whole
stained
planet dreamed.

·

My grandmother, as a teenager,
had the guts to leave

Spain, and never see her parents again —

arriving in America
to her shame

she could not read. O you taught by

deprivation
that your soul is flawed: —

to her shame she could not read.

·

Olive-skinned, bewilderingly
dark, in this California surrounded

everywhere by the brown-skinned

dirt-poor progeny of those her ancestors
conquered and enslaved, she insisted we are

Spanish. Not Mexican. Spanish-Basque.

·

Disconsolate to learn her
seven-year-old grandson

spent the afternoon visiting the house —

had entered, had
eaten at the house —

of his new black friend, her fury

the coward grandson sixty-five years
later cannot from his nerves erase.

·

Or the rage with which she stopped her

daughter from marrying a Lebanese
doctor whose skin was

too dark. Actual Spain

was poverty and humiliation so
deep she refused to discuss it—

or, later, richer, to return.

But the Spanish her only
daughter, my mother, divorced, light-

skinned, spoke

was pure
Castilian. On her walls, the dead world

she loathed and obeyed

kept vigil
from large oval dark oak frames.

·

The terrifying land the whole stained
planet dreamed unstained

Europe first imagined. To me, as a child,
Europe was my grandmother—

clinging to what had
cost her everything, she thought

the mutilations exacted by
discriminations of color

rooted in the stars. We brought
here what we had.

GLUTTON

Ropes of my dead
grandmother's unreproducible

sausage, curing for weeks

on the front porch. My mother,
thoroughly

Americanized, found them

vaguely shameful.
Now though I

taste and taste

I can't find that
taste I so loved as a kid.

Each thing generates the Idea

of itself, the perfect thing that it
is, of course, not—

once, a pear so breathtakingly

succulent I couldn't
breathe. I take back that

"of course."

It's got to be out there again,—
. . . *I have tasted it.*

Once, crossing the Alps by car at night, the great glacier suddenly
   there in the moonlight next to the car, in the silence

alone with it.

                    •

I heard Robert Viscusi read only once, on a rainy night in
   Manhattan.

At the end of a long evening, he read the final lines of the first
   poem in the first *Leaves of Grass*, before the poems had titles.

He read with a still, unmelodramatic directness and simplicity
   that made the lines seem as if distilled from the throat of the
   generous gods.

Early Whitman's eerie equilibrium staring as if adequately at war's
carnage, love's carnage, —

                    •

. . . suspended, I listen.

                    •

This is the departing
sun, distributing its gifts to the earth as it disengages from earth

without grief.

Elation as the hand disengages from its consequence, as the
                                             sovereign soul
charmed by its evanescence

toys with and mocks the expectations of worlds.

As you listen, you think this inaccessible
exultation indifferent to catastrophe's etiology or end

is wisdom.

·

A poem read aloud is by its nature a vision of its nature.

Vision you cannot now reenter, from which when you sound the
    words within later unaided and alone, you are expelled.

2. SOUNDINGS

Soundings of the world, testings
later forgotten but within whose

corpses you then burrowed, feeding: wounds

that taught the inverse of what adults
asserted, even thought they believed: taught

you do not have to hold on tight

to what you love, its nature
is not ever to release you: each testing, each

sounding of the world

one more transparent drop
fallen over your eye and hardening

there, to make you what you secretly

think by trial you have become: perfect
eyeball, observer

without a master. (Untranscendental

disgusted-with-lies
homemade American boy's eyeball.)

•

Each creature must

himself, you were sure, *grind the lens*
through which he perceives the world.

•

Illusion of mastery the boy could not

sustain. Now you have no image, no
recollection of incidents, people,

humiliations, that showed you how

small, absurd you were—
but as if, in all things human, hegemony

breeds loathing

soon all you can see is that the dependent,
hungry, rage-ridden

brain you inhabit

is not a lens, not a prism you have
flawlessly honed that transmits

light, but this suffocating

bubble that encases you, partial, mortal,
stained with the creature that created it.

•

You are the creature that created it.

You You You you cried, reaching
for a knife

to cut through the bubble

smelling of you. The corpses on which
you had so long

fed, turned their faces toward you—;

priests, they said, you must invite
priests to surround you.

.

The question became not
whether a master, but which.

You schooled and reschooled

yourself to bind with
briars your joys and desires.

.

This. Before a series of glamorous or

pure, compellingly severe
chimeras that mastered

the chaos I perceived within and without

all my life I have
implored: —

This. *REMAKE ME* in the image of this.

3.

your gaze, Walt Whitman, through its
mastery of paper

paper on which you invented the illusion of your voice

the intricacies of whose candor and ambition
disarm me

into imagining this is your voice

fueled by the ruthless gaze that
unshackled the chains shackling

queer me in adolescence

(unshackled me maybe for three days
during which I tried to twist out of

knowing what you made me see I knew

and could not bear that I knew
immured in an America that betrayed

the America you taught still must exist)

Ginsberg called you lonely old
courage teacher

but something in young electric you

was before the end
broken

wary alerted listening buck

that seeing all
cannot see or imagine

itself broken

the melancholy spectacle
through your

mastery of paper

as you entirely predicted
transformed into the gaze of others

•

The event, or many mini-events, only implicitly recorded in a poem.

After his father's death but before dressing the mutilated bodies of soldiers, as he walked the shore-line touching debris, flotsam, pierced by his own evanescence everywhere assaulting him, by "the old thought of likenesses,"

your own sweet sole self like debris smashed beneath your feet at the sea's edge,

as he walked there, the old exultant gaze, like an animal's poise, was gone.

But impossible to face becoming detritus, impossible to face it naked, without armor, without ideas about Idea, America, song about Song,

impossible to smell the breath of death without visions, broken, makeshift, aiming at an eloquence that so insinuates, so dyes each vision with the presence, the voice of the singer,

we who have seen what we see through his sight are his progeny,

impossible to face death without progeny as spar on which to cling.

Robert Viscusi, the bullet you aimed at *Leaves of Grass* bounced off its spine and landed, hot, intact, where I now still sit.

FOUR

THREE TATTOOS

Maria Forever

labyrinthine intricate
coiling pent dragon

B R A D

.

gaudy skin prophesying
the fate of the heart

reminder that if you once

cross me
I can destroy you

indelible capital letters

written in flesh to remind
flesh what flesh has forgotten

.

It must be lifted from the mind

must be lifted and placed elsewhere
must not remain in the mind alone

AS YOU CRAVE SOUL

but find flesh
till flesh

almost seems sufficient

when the as-yet-unwritten
poem within you

demands existence

all you can offer it are words. Words
are flesh. Words

are flesh

craving to become idea, idea
dreaming it has found, this time, a body

obdurate as stone.

To carve the body of the world
and out of flesh make flesh

obdurate as stone.

Looking down into the casket-crib
of your love, embittered by

soul you crave to become stone.

You mourn not
what is not, but what never could have been.

What could not ever find a body

because what you wanted, he
wanted but did not want.

Ordinary divided unsimple heart.

What you dream is that, by eating
the flesh of words, what you make

makes mind and body

one. When, after a reading, you are asked
to describe your aesthetics,

you reply, *An aesthetics of embodiment.*

THINGS FALLING FROM GREAT HEIGHTS

Spasm of vision you crave like a secular pentecost

The subject of this poem
is how much the spaces that you now move in

cost

the spaces that you were
given

were born to and like an animal used but then ran from

ran from but then thought you had
transformed

enough to accede to

the choices you made to inhabit the spaces where you
when prompted repeat the story of how you arrived

they cost your life

O RUIN O HAUNTED

O ruin O haunted
restless remnant of

two bodies, two

histories
you felt the unceasing

force of

but never understood,—
terrified that without an

x-ray, a topography of

their souls
you must repeat their lives.

                    •

You did not repeat their lives.

You lodged your faith
in Art—

which gives us

pattern, process
with the flesh

still stuck to it.

With flesh, you
told yourself, pattern

is truer, subtler, less

given to the illusion
seeing frees you from it.

.

Or, you did repeat their lives, —

. . . repeated them by
inverting them.

How you hurtled yourself against, how

cunningly you
failed to elude love.

.

Love
is the manna

that falling

makes you
see

the desert

surrounding you
is a desert.

Makes you think dirt is not where you were born.

PLEA AND CHASTISEMENT

When the exact intonation with which
at the sink she said

"Honey"

at last can sound in no one's head
she will become merely the angry

poems written by an angry son

•

"Honey"

•

which is a cry not about something she must
wash or my latest frightening improvidence

but another wound made by my failure of love

which must flatten the world unless I
forgive her for what in an indecipherable

past she fears she *somehow* did to cause this

•

At five
thrillingly I won the Oedipal struggle

first against my father then stepfather

In our alliance against the world
we were more like each other

than anyone else

till adolescence and the world
showed me this was prison

•

Out of immense appetite we make

immense promises
the future dimensions of which

we cannot see

then see
when it seems death to keep them

•

I can still hear her
"Honey"

plea and chastisement

•

long since become the pillars of the earth
the price exacted

at the door to the dimensional world

MARTHA YARNOZ BIDART HALL

Though she whom you had so let
in, the desire for survival will not

allow you ever to admit
another so deeply in again

Though she, *in*, went crazy
vengeful-crazy

so that, as in Dante, there she ate your heart

Though her house that she despised but
spent her life constructing

still cannot, thirty-nine years after
her death, by your ratiocination or rage

be uncon-
structed

you think, *We had an encounter on the earth*

each of us
hungry beyond belief

As long as you are alive
she is alive

You are the leaping
dog

capricious on the grass, lunging
at something only it can see.

LATE FAIRBANKS

As in his early films, still the old
abandon, a mischievous, blithe ardor.

Through unending repetition, it became
part of his muscles.

To leap
push

against earth
and spring.

But the ground under him has changed.
He doesn't remember when it happened.

When he wasn't looking
the earth turned to mush.

AGAINST RAGE

He had not been denied the world. Terrible
scenes that he clung to because they taught him

the world will at last be buried with him.
As well as the exhilarations. Now,

he thinks each new one will be the last one.
The last new page. The last sex. *Each human*

being's story, he tells nobody, *is a boat*
cutting through the night. As starless blackness

approaches, the soul reverses itself, in
the eerie acceptance of finitude.

FOR THE AIDS DEAD

The plague you have thus far survived. They didn't.
Nothing that they did in bed that you didn't.

Writing a poem, I cleave to "you." You
means I, one, you, as well as the you

inside you constantly talk to. Without
justice or logic, without

sense, you survived. They didn't.
Nothing that they did in bed that you didn't.

TYRANT

In this journey through flesh
not just in flesh or with flesh

but through it

you drive forward seeing
in the rearview mirror

seeing only

there
always growing smaller

what you drive toward

What you drive toward
is what you once made with flesh

Out of stone caulked with blood

mortared
with blood and flesh

you made a house

bright now in the rearview mirror
white in the coarse sun's coarse light

No more men died making it

than any other ruthless
monument living men admire

Now as your body betrays you

what you made with flesh
is what you must drive toward

what you must before

you die reassure
teach yourself you made

The house mortared with flesh

as if defying the hand of its
maker

when you pull up to it at last

dissolves as it has always
dissolved

In this journey through flesh

not just in flesh or with flesh
but through flesh

MOUTH

It was as if, starving, his stomach
rebelled at food, *as quickly as he ate*
it passed right through him, his body
refused what his body needed. Recipe
for death. *But,*
he said, *what others think is food isn't food.*
It passed right through him, he shoved
meat into his mouth but still his
body retained nothing. Absorbed
nothing. He grows
thinner. He thinks he cannot live on
nothing. He has the persistent
sense that whatever object he seeks
is not what he seeks, —
. . . now he repeats the litany of his choices.
Love, which always to his surprise
exhilarated even as it tormented
and absorbed him. Unendingly under
everything, art—; trying to make
a work of art he can continue to inhabit.
The choices he made he said he made
almost without choosing.
The best times, I must confess, are when
one cannot help oneself.
Has his pride at his intricate
inventions come to nothing?
Nothing he can now name or touch is food.

Sex was the bed where you learned to be
naked and not naked at the same time.
Bed
where you learned to move the unsustainable
weight inside, then too often
lost the key to it.
Faces too close, that despite themselves
promise, then out of panic disappoint.
Not just out of panic; only in his mind
is he freely both *here* and *not here*. The imperious
or imagined needs of those you
love or think you love
demand you forget that when you smell your
flesh you smell
unfulfilment.
We are creatures, he thinks, caught in an obscure,
ruthless economy, —
. . . his hunger
grows as whatever his mouth fastens upon
fails to feed him. Recipe
for death. But he's sure he'll learn something
once he sees
La Notte again. He's placed *Duino Elegies*
next to his bed. He craves the cold
catechism Joyce mastered writing "Ithaca."
Now he twists within the box
he cannot exit or rise above.
He thinks he must die
when what will not allow him to retain food
makes him see his body has disappeared.

I am here to fix the door.

Use has almost destroyed it. Disuse
would have had the same effect.

No, you're not confused, you didn't
call. If you call you still have hope.

Now you think you have
lived past the necessity for doors.

Carmen Miranda
is on the TV, inviting you to Rio.

Go to sleep while I fix the door.

PRESAGE

Here, at the rim of what has not yet
been, the monotonous

I want to die sung

over and over by your
soul to your soul

just beneath sound

which you once again fail
not to hear, cannot erase or obliterate

returns you to the mirror of itself: —

Mumps, Meningitis, Encephalitis
all at once, together, at

age eight or nine —

•

(later, for months, you dragged your left
leg as you walked, that's what everyone

told you because you hadn't noticed, you

were undersea, the entire
perceptual world

undersea, death your new

familiar, like the bright slime-
green bile you watched for days

inexorably pumped from your stomach)

.

or, later, at thirteen, TYPHOID,
when the doctors said the next two days

will decide if you live, or die—;

you tried, very calmly, to ask yourself
whether you did actually want to live,

the answer, you knew, not clear—

then you heard
something say

I want to live, despite the metaphysical

awfulness of this incontinent
body shitting uncontrollably into a toilet in

time, this place, blind self, hobbled, hobbling animal,—

•

You are undersea. These are not entwined
ropes, but thick twisted slime-green

cables. Laid out before you is the fabled
Gordian knot, which you must cut.

Which you must cut not
to rule the earth, but escape it.

All you must do is sever them. Your blade
breaks, as the ties that bind thicken, tighten.

ELEGY FOR EARTH

Because earth's inmates travel in flesh

and hide from flesh

and adore flesh

you hunger for flesh that does not die

But hunger for the absolute
breeds hatred of the absolute

Those who are the vessels of revelation

or who think that they are

ravage

us with the promise of rescue

       •

My mother outside in the air
waving, shriveled, as if she knew

this is the last time —

watching as I climbed the stairs
and the plane swallowed me. She and I

could no more change what we hurtled toward

than we could change the weather. Finding my
seat, unseen I stared back as she receded.

.

They drop into holes in the earth, everything

you loved, loved and
hated, as you will drop —

and the moment when all was possible

gone. You are still
above earth, the moment when all

and nothing is possible

long gone. Terrified of the sea, we
cling to the hull.

.

In adolescence, you thought your work
ancient work: to decipher at last

human beings' relation to God. Decipher

love. To make what was once whole
whole again: or to see

why it never should have been thought whole.

•

Earth was a tiny labyrinthine ball orbiting

another bigger ball
so bright

you can go blind staring at it

when the source of warmth and light
withdraws

then terrible winter

when burning and relentless
it draws too close

the narcotically gorgeous

fecund earth
withers

as if the sun

as if the sun
taught us

what we will ever know of the source

now too
far

then too close

.

Blood

island
where you for a time lived

FIVE

OF HIS BONES ARE CORAL MADE

He still trolled books, films, gossip, his own
past, searching not just for

ideas that dissect the mountain that

in his early old age he is almost convinced
cannot be dissected:

he searched for stories:

stories the pattern of whose
knot dimly traces the pattern of his own:

what is intolerable in

the world, which is to say
intolerable in himself, ingested, digested:

the stories that

haunt each of us, for each of us
rip open the mountain.

•

the creature smothered in death clothes

dragging into the forest
bodies he killed to make meaning

the woman who found that she

to her bewilderment and horror
had a body

      •

As if certain algae

that keep islands of skeletons
alive, that make living rock from

trash, from carcasses left behind by others,

as if algae
were to produce out of

themselves and what they most fear

the detritus over whose
kingdom they preside: the burning

fountain is the imagination

within us that ingests and by its
devouring generates

what is most antithetical to itself:

it returns the intolerable as
brilliant dream, visible, opaque,

teasing analysis:

makes from what you find hardest to
swallow, most indigestible, your food.

POEM ENDING WITH A SENTENCE BY HEATH LEDGER

Each grinding flattened American vowel smashed to
centerlessness, his glee that whatever long ago mutilated his

mouth, he has mastered to mutilate

you: the Joker's voice, so unlike
the bruised, withheld, wounded voice of Ennis Del Mar.

Once I have the voice

that's
the line

and at

the end
of the line

is a hook

and attached
to that

is the soul.

DREAM REVEALS IN NEON THE GREAT ADDICTIONS

LOVE, with its simulacrum, sex.

The words, like a bonfire encased
in glass, glowed on the horizon.

POWER, with its simulacrum, money.

FAME, with its simulacrum, celebrity.

GOD, survived
by what survives belief, the desire to be

a Saint.

Seed of your obsessions, these are
the addictions that tempt your soul.

Then, seeing the word ART, I woke.

•

Refused love, power, fame, sainthood, your
tactic, like that of modest

Caesar, is to feign indifference and refusal.
You are addicted to what you cannot possess.

You cannot tell if
addictions, secret, narcotic,

damage or enlarge
mind, through which you seize the world.

GANYMEDE

On this earth where no secure foothold is,
deathbound.

You're deathbound. You can't stop moving when you're
at rest.

Transfixed by your destination, by what
you fear

you want. *Unlike each bright scene, bright thing, each*
nervous

dumb sweet creature whose death you mourn, you will
not die.

Chimera to whose voice even Jesus
succumbed.

How you loathed crawling on the earth seeing
nothing.

When the god pulled you up into the air,
taking

you showed you you wanted to be taken.

ON THIS EARTH WHERE NO SECURE FOOTHOLD IS

Wanting to be a movie star like Dean Stockwell or Gigi Perreau, answering an ad at ten or eleven you made your mother drive you to Hollywood and had expensive Hollywood pictures taken.

•

Hollywood wasn't buying.

•

Everyone is buying but not everyone wants to buy you.

•

You see the kids watching, brooding.

•

Religion, politics, love, work, sex—each enthrallment, each enthusiasm presenting itself as pleasure or necessity, is recruitment.

•

Each kid is at the edge of a sea.

·

At each kid's feet multitudinous voices say *I will buy you if you buy me.*

·

Who do you want to be bought by?

·

The child learns this is the question almost immediately.

·

Mother?

·

Father?

·

Both mother and father tried to enlist you but soon you learned that you couldn't enlist on both sides at the same time.

·

They lied that you could but they were at war and soon you learned you couldn't.

•

How glamorous they were!

•

As they aged they mourned that to buyers they had become invisible.

•

Both of them in the end saw beneath them only abyss.

•

You are at the edge of a sea.

•

You want to buy but you know not everyone wants to buy you.

•

Each enthrallment is recruitment.

•

Your body will be added to the bodies that piled-up make the structures of the world.

·

Your body will be erased, swallowed.

·

Who do you want to be swallowed by?

·

It's almost the same question as To be or not to be.

·

Figuring out who they want to be bought by is what all the kids with brooding looks on their face are brooding about.

·

Your weapon is your mind.

FOR AN UNWRITTEN OPERA

Once you had a secret love: seeing
even his photo, a window is flung open
high in the airless edifice that is you.

Though everything looks as if it is continuing
just as before, it is not, it is continuing
in a new way (sweet lingo O'Hara and Ashbery

teach). That's not how you naturally speak:
you tell yourself, first, that he is not the air
you need; second, that you loathe air.

As a boy you despised the world for replacing
God with another addiction, love.
Despised yourself. Was there no third thing?

But every blue moon the skeptical, the adamantly
disabused find themselves, like you,
returned to life by a secret: like him, in you.

Now you understand Janáček at
seventy, in love with a much younger
married woman, chastely writing her.

As in Mozart song remains no matter how
ordinary, how flawed the personae. For us poor
mortals: private accommodations. Magpie beauty.

NOTES

"Writing 'Ellen West'" (p. 4). "The Case of Ellen West" by Ludwig Binswanger is included in *Existence*, edited by Rollo May, Ernest Angel, and Henri F. Ellenberger, translated by Werner M. Mendel and Joseph Lyons (Basic Books, 1958). My poem "Ellen West" appears in *The Book of the Body* (1977), collected in *In the Western Night: Collected Poems 1965–90*.

The gestures poems make are the same as the gestures of ritual injunction — curse; exorcism; prayer; underlying everything perhaps, the attempt to make someone or something live again. Both poet and shaman make a model that stands for the whole. Substitution, symbolic substitution. The mind conceives that something lived, or might live. Implicit is the demand to understand. The memorial that is ward and warning. Without these ancient springs poems are merely more words.

"Defrocked" (p. 25). In the first section, the anonymous lyrics are quoted from Evelyn Underhill's *Mysticism* (Chapter VI, section I), except for "*pilgrimage to a cross in the void*," from Ginsberg's *Howl* (Part III).

"Threnody on the Death of Harriet Smithson" (p. 41). This is a kind of fantasia based on an essay by Jules Janin (*The Memoirs of Hector Berlioz*, translated by David Cairns). Smithson was an actress, and became the wife of Berlioz.

"Dream of the Book" (p. 45). The passage ending with "unbroken but in stasis" uses a sentence from Lionel Trilling's essay "Art and Fortune" (*The Liberal Imagination*, 1950). The sentence is quoted in full in the interview with Mark Halliday at the end of *In the Western Night: Collected Poems 1965–90*.

"Whitman" (p. 57). "The old thought of likenesses" is from "As I Ebb'd with the Ocean of Life," first published in 1860; the version of *Leaves of Grass* discussed at the beginning of my poem appeared five years earlier, in 1855. Whitman revised and enlarged *Leaves of Grass* for the rest of his life.

"Martha Yarnoz Bidart Hall" (p. 78). "As in Dante, there she ate your heart" refers to the first sonnet in *La Vita Nuova*. There is a very free version in *Desire* (1997) titled "Love Incarnate."

"Mouth" (p. 85). The two lines beginning *"The best times"* are based on words by Otto Klemperer, *Klemperer on Music* (Toccata Press, 1986, p. 21). *La Notte* is the film by Michelangelo Antonioni. "Ithaca" is the next-to-last chapter of *Ulysses*.

"Presage" (p. 88). The prophecy about the Gordian knot was that the person who succeeded in untying it would rule Asia. Alexander the Great, newly arrived in Asia, did not untie it but cut through it.

"Of His Bones Are Coral Made" (p. 97). This statement appeared with the poem in *Best American Poetry 2012*:

> I've written little prose about poetry, but can't seem to stop writing poems about poetics. Narrative is the Elephant in the Room when most people discuss poetry. Narrative was never a crucial element in the poetics surrounding the birth of Modernism, though the great works of Modernism, from *The Waste Land* to the *Cantos* to "Home Burial," *Paterson* and beyond, are built on a brilliant sense of the power of narrative. What Modernism added was the power gained when you know what to leave out. Narrative is the ghost scaffolding that gives spine to the great works that haunt the twentieth century.
>
> A writer is caught by certain narratives, certain characters, and not by others. Prufrock is relevant to our sense of Eliot. He could be a character in Pound's sequence "Hugh Selwyn Mauberley," but if he were, it would be without the identification, the sympathy and agony. Eliot had to go on to Gerontion and Sweeney and Tiresias, each trailing a ghost narrative.

They are as crucial to the vision of Eliot as Bloom and Stephen Dedalus are to the vision, the sense of the nature of the world, of Joyce.

In my poem, "the creature smothered in death clothes" is Herbert White, the title character in the first poem in my first book; "the woman" two stanzas down is Ellen West, from the second.

Two more allusions. "The burning fountain" refers to this passage in Shelley's "Adonais," his elegy for Keats:

> He wakes or sleeps with the enduring dead;
> Thou canst not soar where he is sitting now.
> Dust to the dust: but the pure spirit shall flow
> Back to the burning fountain whence it came,
> A portion of the Eternal, which must glow
> Through time and change, unquenchably the same . . .

"The burning fountain"—the power that fuels, that generates and animates life—is the title of a book about the poetic imagination by Philip Wheelwright, whose classes I took as an undergraduate (*The Burning Fountain*, Indiana University Press, 1954).

My poem's title comes from Shakespeare's *The Tempest*:

> Full fathom five thy father lies;
>   Of his bones are coral made;
> Those are pearls that were his eyes:
>   Nothing of him that doth fade,
> But doth suffer a sea-change
> Into something rich and strange.

My poem is about transformation, the bones of the poet made up out of the materials, the detritus of the world, that he or she has not only gathered but transformed and been transformed by.

"Poem Ending with a Sentence by Heath Ledger" (p. 100). The Joker (in *The Dark Knight*) and Ennis Del Mar (in *Brokeback Mountain*) are Ledger's greatest roles.

INTERVIEW WITH FRANK BIDART

Conducted by Shara Lessley for the National Book Foundation, October 2013

Shara Lessley: In an effort to promote a literary event in Bakersfield, a woman once rented a billboard that read FRANK BIDART IS COMING HOME. Although you've been gone from California for some time, there are poems in *Metaphysical Dog* that return there. Is there a part of you that still inhabits the Golden State?

Frank Bidart: The person who did that was a writer named Lee McCarthy, who taught high school near Bakersfield. She was terrifically gutsy, independent, courageous. She was angry that I had been left out of a semi-official anthology of California poets. She invited me to read in Bakersfield, and arranged for the billboard to startle anyone driving by.

   Though I've now lived in New England much longer than my years growing up in Bakersfield, I've never thought of myself as a New Englander. I'm deeply someone made in California, in Bakersfield. Elizabeth Bishop has a wonderful line, "Home-made, home-made! But aren't we all?" But if you make yourself in California it's different than if you make yourself in Massachusetts. Class issues and assumptions, racial issues, manners are different. The things you argue about in your head are different. I think the things that are "Californian" about me have been modified as I've gotten older, but haven't changed in essence. Though everything I've written has been an argument with the world I'm from, I'm no less a creature of it. This is an enormous, labyrinthine subject, as it probably is for any writer who felt wounded but made by the place he or she began. Think of Joyce and Ireland.

SL: Hunger in *Metaphysical Dog* is exhausting but persistent. "Words / are flesh," you write. The collection's speakers crave the soul, the absolute. Is desire for "the great addictions"—love, power, fame, God, and art—a flaw? Or, is it simply what drives what you call the "Ordinary divided unsimple heart"?

FB: I think they are what drive the ordinary divided unsimple heart. Though it's terrible to give in unqualifiedly to the desire for them, the notion that one has eradicated them from oneself—or that you should be ashamed you feel them—is naive, an illusion, one more chimera. No matter who or what you are, possessing whatever social or economic stature you've been born into or achieved, hunger is universal—hunger for something you don't possess, once thought important. Everyone feels grief for the unlived life. But not every addiction is equal. I tell my students that it's better to be addicted to Astaire and Rogers movies than to heroin. The notion that, short of death, one is going to be totally free of addictions is one more way of torturing oneself.

SL: "Writing 'Ellen West'" revisits your well-known poem on anorexia. Like Ellen, you claim, "*he* was / obsessed with eating and the arbitrariness of gender and having to / have a body" (emphasis mine). As a narrative strategy, why transform yourself into a character via the third person?

FB: It's a way of making fact available to art. To write about oneself as a character—to think about oneself as a character—opens up space between the "I" and the author. (In this sense, calling the *I* "he" is only a way of making inescapable this space. You can write as an "I" and still think of yourself as a character.) The space is necessary because the work isn't going to be any good if it is merely a subtle form of self-justification, if one is supine before the romance of the self. Not that self-justification is ever wholly absent.

SL: Image is often exploited as a means of generating feeling or propelling the contemporary poem's plot. *Metaphysical Dog*, in contrast, is stark—it draws its energy primarily from abstraction and pattern-making. Do ideas incite your work rather than concrete details?

FB: What's crucial for any writer is to understand how your mind apprehends meaning. How, in your experience, you apprehend significance. Understand it and find a way to embody it, make it have the force for the reader in a work of art that it has for you. Images, what the eye sees, are of course part of this for everyone. But I think tone of voice, situation, the look in an eye or on a face, are as much part of what make up for me "meaning" as what traditionally people think of as "images." When Williams said, "no ideas but in things," that's not an image. Pound's "Down, Derry-down / Oh let an old man rest," is not an image. Pound was of course right when he said, "Go in fear of abstractions." Abstractions can smother the quick of feeling in a poem. But reaching for abstractions and conceiving abstractions are not separable from feeling for a human being. When Williams said, "no ideas but in things," he didn't mean "no ideas."

SL: I'm struck by how precisely the last ten lines of "Poem Ending with a Sentence by Heath Ledger" characterize your life's work:

Once I have the voice

that's
the line

and at

the end
of the line

is a hook

and attached
to that

is the soul.

How are you able to imagine and sustain such varied voices—the sweeping dramatic monologues of your early collections, for instance, versus the more intimate lyric and philosophical poems that populate *Metaphysical Dog*?

FB: First of all, that sentence really *is* by Heath Ledger. When I saw it printed in an interview, it was printed simply as prose. But I thought there was a movement in it, an iron logic if you will, that would be apprehended if it was set up in lines. I struggled over and over to do so. I found that this movement was apprehensible if I used a form that I have more and more used the longer I've written: a single line followed by a two-line stanza, followed by another single line followed by a two-line stanza. One followed by two followed by one followed by two. I've found this form tremendously flexible; it reveals the anatomy of many (but not all) sentences that, for me, are eloquent. One magazine that printed the poem—a magazine that did not send me proofs—eliminated all the stanza breaks, in an attempt to save space. The poem was reduced to drivel. It's how the words exist in space that allows them, on the page, their eloquence.

Crucial to getting a character to speak in a poem is hearing in your head as you write the way the character talks. Because a poem is made up of words, speech *is* how the soul is embodied. (Ledger asserts, of course, that even in a movie this is true.) What's crucial is that how the words are set down on the page not muffle the voice. When I first began writing, writing the voice down in the ways conventional in contemporary practice seemed to muffle or kill the voice I still heard in my head. If I lost that voice, I knew I had lost everything. I'm grateful to Ledger for saying more succinctly than I have ever been able to what I had felt since I began writing.

SL: "I don't know the value of what I've written," said Robert Lowell, "but I know that I changed the game." Your poems—with their typographical innovations, mining of the paradoxical, psychological complexity—have been game-changers for so many of us. What about your own work or the process of making poems continues to surprise you?

FB: Nothing is better about writing than the passages about writing in Eliot's *Four Quartets*. "A raid on the inarticulate / With shabby equipment always deteriorating . . . / the intolerable wrestle / With words and meanings." The solutions that I felt I found aren't going to be the solutions that work for someone else. But I'll be happy if my poems seem to say to younger writers that you still can be as bold about setting a poem down on the page as Wordsworth was or Mallarmé was or Ben Jonson was or Pound was or Ginsberg and Lowell and Bishop were. Getting the dynamics and voice down are what's crucial. Whatever it takes to get the whole soul into a poem. An emphasis on voice isn't fashionable in contemporary practice. I hope my poems make people reconsider that.